The Department of Education's Office for Civil Rights (OCR) protects the rights of persons with disabilities under two federal laws. One of these is Section 504 of the Rehabilitation Act of 1973, which prohibits discrimination based on disability in programs and activities operated by recipients of federal funds. It states: "No otherwise qualified individual with a disability in the United States...shall, solely by reason of her or his disability, be excluded from the participation in, be denied the benefits of, or be subjected to discrimination under any program or activity receiving Federal financial assistance..."[1]

> "In schools, the workplace, and throughout our public life, we are committed to ensuring that people with disabilities have an equal chance at achieving the American dream."
>
> —Secretary Arne Duncan, July 26, 2012

The other law is Title II of the Americans with Disabilities Act of 1990 (ADA), which prohibits discrimination based on disability by public entities, regardless of whether they receive federal financial assistance. Title II states: "[N]o qualified individual with a disability shall, by reason of such disability, be excluded from participation in or be denied the benefits of the services, programs, or activities of a public entity, or be subjected to discrimination by any such entity."[2]

What is a disability?

Section 504 and Title II do not contain a specified list of disabilities. Instead, they use a functional definition of disability. Under this approach, a person has a disability if he or she: (1) has a physical or mental impairment that substantially limits one or more major life activities of that person; (2) has a record of such an impairment; or (3) is regarded as having such an impairment. Congress has made clear that the definition of disability should be understood to allow for broad coverage. A few examples of impairments that can be disabilities are blindness, deafness, orthopedic impairments, autism, learning disabilities, Attention-Deficit Disorder (ADD) and Attention-Deficit/Hyperactivity Disorder (ADHD), diabetes, food allergies, HIV and AIDS, and depression.

OCR enforces Section 504 in all elementary and secondary schools, colleges and universities, and other educational institutions – public or private – that receive federal financial assistance from the Department. OCR, along with the Department of Justice, enforces Title II at all public educational institutions, including public elementary and secondary schools, colleges and universities, as well as at public libraries. The protections of Section 504 and Title II, which are generally the same in the context of education, cover all aspects of these institutions' programs and activities. Both laws cover school districts of all sizes, and traditional public schools as well as public charter schools.

The goal of these disability civil rights laws is to provide equal opportunity and fundamental fairness for students with disabilities, including access to special education and related aids and services at public elementary and secondary schools; academic adjustments at colleges and universities; accessible technology; accessible programs, services and facilities; and the right to equal treatment and benefits.

A hallmark of these laws is that, in order to ensure that equal opportunity is provided to students with disabilities and to avoid discriminating on the basis of disability, the laws require schools, colleges and universities to sometimes treat students with disabilities differently from students without disabilities. Another hallmark is the imperative to address the particular needs of each student with a disability. Thus, these laws recognize that not only are there many different disabilities, but students with the same disability may not have the same needs.

As we observe the 39th anniversary of Section 504 on September 26, 2012, we celebrate our nation's progress in the area of disability rights in education. We also recognize that equal opportunity for people with disabilities has not yet been achieved. Section 504 and Title II, along with the Individuals with Disabilities Education Act (IDEA), administered by the Department's Office of Special Education Programs (see sidebar on next page), demonstrate our nation's commitment to providing quality education to all students with disabilities. To honor that commitment, OCR will continue to vigorously enforce Section 504 and Title II to ensure that students with disabilities receive the education that all students deserve.

Section 504 and the Individuals with Disabilities Education Act

The Individuals with Disabilities Education Act (IDEA) is a federal law that provides federal funds for special education and sets requirements for such services. IDEA is administered by the Department of Education's Office of Special Education Programs (OSEP) in the Office of Special Education and Rehabilitative Services (OSERS). More information about IDEA is available at http://idea.ed.gov/.

Some students with disabilities are covered by Section 504 and Title II but not by IDEA. This is because IDEA is limited to students who need special education, while Section 504 and Title II apply to all students with disabilities, including those who do not need special education but may require some other aids and services. Students with disabilities who are covered by Section 504 but not by IDEA are sometimes referred to as "504-only" students. For example, a student with diabetes who does not need special education but does need assistance administering insulin would be such a "504-only" student. While OCR does not enforce IDEA, OCR does enforce the Section 504 and Title II rights of IDEA-protected students.

OCR has worked diligently to ensure the protections of Section 504 and Title II in schools and colleges. In doing so, we have used the following tools:

POLICY GUIDANCE: OCR issues detailed policy guidance documents to help schools and colleges, as well as students, parents, and members of the public, understand what the civil rights laws, including Section 504 and Title II, require. These documents, which OCR sends to institutions around the country and posts on the OCR website, address the legal requirements and considerations governing situations frequently encountered by schools and colleges. The documents provide guidelines for how such institutions can meet their legal obligations. Since January 2009, OCR has issued four guidance documents that address topics related to disability rights: (1) equal access to electronic book readers and other technology for post-secondary students with disabilities; (2) equal access to emerging technologies for all students, including elementary and secondary school students; (3) schools' obligations to respond to bullying and harassment based on disability; and (4) changes in the meaning of "disability" made by the ADA Amendments Act of 2008.

ENFORCEMENT: OCR investigates allegations of discrimination filed with our regional offices and, as needed, obtains robust remedies that address the root causes of the discrimination. Almost 600 OCR team members lead this work from our headquarters and 12 regional offices around the country.

COMPLAINTS AND PROACTIVE INVESTIGATIONS: In the fiscal years 2009 through 2011,[3] OCR received over 11,700 disability-related complaints – more than ever before in a three-year period. While OCR enforces civil rights laws that prohibit discrimination based on race, color, national origin, sex, and age, as well as disability, a large portion of our overall work involves disability complaints: more than 55 percent of the complaints OCR received during this period raised disability issues. In addition, in the last three fiscal years, OCR launched over 30 systemic, proactive investigations that, collectively, address a broad range of disability-related issues in institutions across the country. OCR has employed innovative techniques to resolve many of these complaints and investigations, often involving multiple stakeholders to design and sustain meaningful change at the institutions involved.

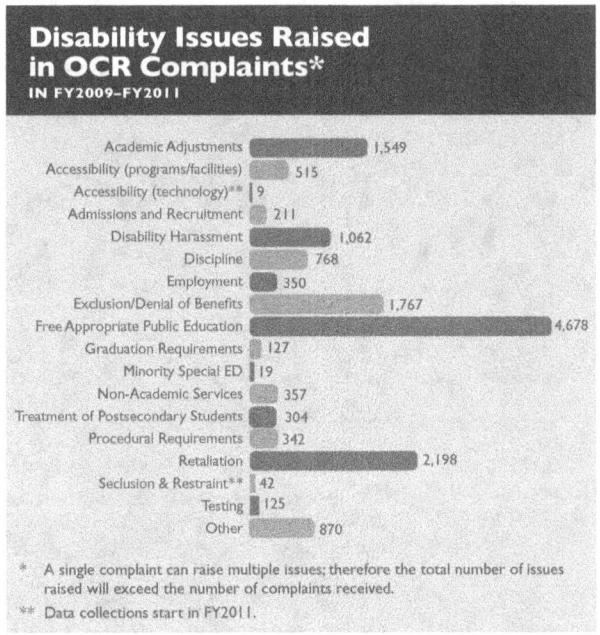

Disability Issues Raised in OCR Complaints*
IN FY2009–FY2011

Issue	Value
Academic Adjustments	1,549
Accessibility (programs/facilities)	515
Accessibility (technology)**	9
Admissions and Recruitment	211
Disability Harassment	1,062
Discipline	768
Employment	350
Exclusion/Denial of Benefits	1,767
Free Appropriate Public Education	4,678
Graduation Requirements	127
Minority Special ED	19
Non-Academic Services	357
Treatment of Postsecondary Students	304
Procedural Requirements	342
Retaliation	2,198
Seclusion & Restraint**	42
Testing	125
Other	870

* A single complaint can raise multiple issues; therefore the total number of issues raised will exceed the number of complaints received.

** Data collections start in FY2011.

TECHNICAL ASSISTANCE: Educators, as well as parents and students, must have the knowledge and skills to identify discrimination, to prevent it, and to address it or get help when it does occur. Every year, OCR provides technical assistance to schools and communities around the country on both longstanding and emerging civil rights issues. In the last three years, OCR has conducted hundreds of disability-related technical assistance presentations, 105 in the first six months of FY 2012 alone.

Protecting the Nation's Wounded Warriors

In the past three years, OCR has conducted numerous technical assistance activities to assist "wounded warriors," such as veterans returning from Operation Iraqi Freedom and Operation Enduring Freedom, who are starting or returning to college. OCR has observed that many veterans who acquired disabilities during their service are unfamiliar with the protections afforded to them under Section 504 and Title II (such as the right to request disability-based accommodations). Similarly, educational institutions are not uniformly prepared to serve an influx of veterans with combat-related disabilities such as Traumatic Brain Injury and Post-Traumatic Stress Disorder. OCR's technical assistance has informed veterans, educators and service providers from institutions such as the Veterans Administration about how the protections afforded to postsecondary students with disabilities apply to those returning from war.

Enforcing Section 504 and Title II

This document highlights a small sample of OCR's disability-related work on the following issues:

- **Free Appropriate Public Education (FAPE):** Ensuring that students with disabilities attending public elementary and secondary schools receive regular or special education and related aids and services so that their needs are met as adequately as those of students without disabilities.
- **Discipline:** Ensuring that students are not inappropriately punished or disciplined for reasons related to their disability and are not subjected to discriminatorily different treatment in discipline.
- **Academic Adjustments:** Ensuring that college students with disabilities receive needed academic modifications and auxiliary aids and services.
- **Accessibility of Technology:** Requiring schools and colleges to use technology that is accessible to individuals with disabilities or to otherwise provide equal access to the educational benefits and opportunities afforded by the technology.

- **Physical Accessibility of Programs, Services and Facilities:** Requiring schools and colleges to make any programs, services and facilities physically accessible to individuals with disabilities.

- **Harassment, Including Bullying that Rises to the Level of Harassment:** Requiring schools and colleges to prevent and address harassment on the basis of disability.

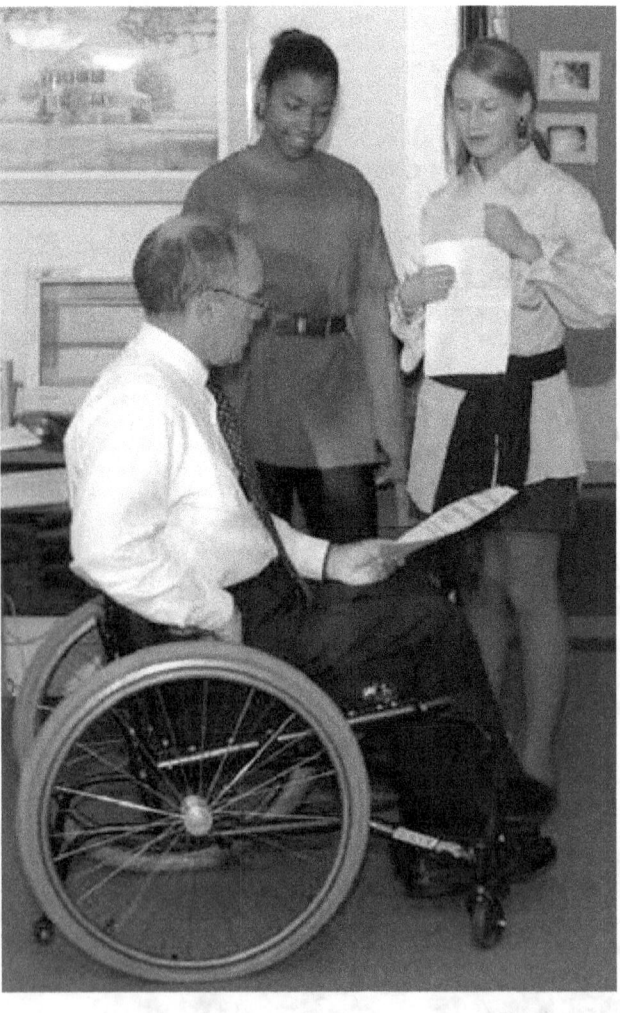

- **Right to Equal Treatment:** Requiring that schools and colleges provide students with disabilities an equal opportunity to participate in, and receive the benefits of, the institutions' programs. This applies to such areas as admissions and recruitment; college and university housing; access to nonacademic and extracurricular activities, including extracurricular athletics; retaliation; and employment.

- **Additional Areas of Focus:** Beyond the issues addressed in this document, OCR routinely handles an array of topics related to disability rights, including graduation requirements; testing accommodations for students with disabilities to ensure that test results accurately reflect the students' aptitude or achievement level; procedural requirements such as schools' and colleges' obligations to publish notices of nondiscrimination, designate and publish information about Section 504 and ADA coordinators, and provide grievance procedures; and the improper restraint and seclusion of students with disabilities that can lead to tragic consequences for students.

- **The Transformed Civil Rights Data Collection:** Providing new information about schools across the country to improve compliance with Section 504 and Title II. The Civil Rights Data Collection, accessible at http://ocrdata.ed.gov, now covers issues such as access to college and career preparatory courses, discipline, harassment and school finances, which can be analyzed and disaggregated by disability, race, ethnicity, English proficiency status and sex.

Free Appropriate Public Education (FAPE)

Children with disabilities have the same right to K–12 public education as children without disabilities. In order to receive and benefit from that education, students with disabilities may need something different -- special education, or perhaps related aids and services -- than students without disabilities. OCR works to ensure that public elementary and secondary schools, including charter schools, provide a free appropriate public education (FAPE) to all "qualified students" with disabilities (generally, students with disabilities who are of school age), regardless of the nature or severity of their disabilities.

Policy Guidance: FAPE

The Department issued policy guidance in 2012 addressing the requirements of Title II and Section 504 in the elementary and secondary school context in light of changes to these laws made by Congress in 2008 that broadened their scope of protection. The guidance explained how, under the amended laws, more students may have a disability and require evaluation to determine whether they need special education or related aids and services.

The guidance also addressed the need for schools to revisit health plans developed for some students. Under the amended laws' broadened definition of disability, more students with conditions such as food allergies, asthma and diabetes may now be covered by Section 504 and Title II. Therefore, schools may need to examine such students' health plans to ensure that schools have met the Section 504 requirements for evaluation, placement, and procedural safeguards.

The Department also worked with the National Diabetes Education Program of the Department of Health and Human Services in updating the program's guidance on how to ensure optimal diabetes management in schools in 2010.[4]

Enforcement: FAPE

In Fiscal Years 2009–11, OCR received over 4,600 complaints alleging FAPE violations. This is by far the disability issue on which OCR receives the most complaints, making up almost two-fifths of the more than 11,700 disability complaints received in this time period. During this same period, OCR launched over 15 proactive systemwide investigations around the country concerning the provision of FAPE.

What is an "appropriate education" under Section 504?

Under Section 504, an "appropriate education" is regular or special education and related aids and services that meet the educational needs of students with disabilities as adequately as the needs of nondisabled students and that satisfy certain procedural requirements. Public schools must evaluate students who, because of a disability, may need special education or related services; determine what those services should be; and provide those services along with procedural safeguards. FAPE requires that students with disabilities be educated with students without disabilities to the maximum extent appropriate to meet the needs of the students with disabilities.

A fast resolution of complaints in this area can allow schools, students and parents to keep their focus on students' education. OCR has special resolution tools that can allow it to resolve many of these cases quickly. OCR's Early Complaint Resolution (ECR) process allows the complainant and the school to find a solution through mediation, often before OCR's investigation has even begun. OCR can also reach an agreement with a school district prior to the conclusion of its investigation.

The following are some of the FAPE issues OCR has addressed recently:

Evaluation and Placement of Students With Disabilities

- **A school district** required parents to obtain, at their own expense, medical documentation

supporting the existence of disabilities for their children. The district also required parents to demonstrate that their children were being discriminated against before it would conduct an evaluation. While school districts can consider information submitted by parents, districts may not require parents to provide diagnostic information or obtain outside assessments of students before conducting an evaluation. Furthermore, the failure to evaluate a student suspected of having a disability is itself discrimination based on disability; school districts may not require parents to demonstrate discrimination before their child is evaluated. Pursuant to its agreement with OCR, the district is revising and training staff on its referral procedures and forms, and reimbursing parents who had paid for evaluations.

- **OCR launched a** proactive investigation to

determine if a school district was appropriately evaluating whether students who had individual health care plans to address food allergies, asthma, diabetes and other health impairments were "qualified students with a disability," as defined by Section 504 and Title II. OCR also investigated whether the district was discriminating against students on the basis of race by denying them the opportunity to receive related aids and services, in violation of Title VI of the Civil Rights Act of 1964. In the resolution obtained by OCR, the district agreed to revise its policies and procedures to ensure the prompt identification, evaluation and placement of students with disabilities, including students with food allergies, diabetes, asthma and other health impairments.

- **A charter school** failed to properly evaluate, in a timely manner, a sixth-grade transfer student with a severe, potentially life-threatening peanut allergy to determine if she had a disability and needed services to receive FAPE. The student had had a Section 504 plan at her previous school. Pursuant to its agreement with OCR, the school committed to evaluating the student to determine if she had a disability and, if so, to developing a Section 504 plan to ensure that she received FAPE and could safely attend school. The school also notified other parents of students with food allergies of their rights under Section 504, and developed and provided training on written policies and procedures consistent with Section 504.

- **OCR has several** open proactive investigations regarding minority students being inappropriately and disproportionately categorized as "mentally retarded" (having an intellectual disability), emotionally disturbed or learning disabled. While this primarily raises issues of discrimination based on race, color or national origin in violation of Title VI of the Civil Rights Act of 1964, it also suggests a failure of school districts to properly refer for evaluation, evaluate, place and serve minority students with disabilities who need special education or related aids and services. One of OCR's approaches in these cases will be to review the FAPE determinations to make sure that minority students with and without disabilities have been properly evaluated and are receiving the appropriate education.

- **OCR facilitated an** Early Complaint Resolution in a case in which parents alleged that the school district had not fully implemented the individualized education program (IEP) developed under IDEA for their child, who had a mood disorder disability. Implementation of an IEP is one means of providing FAPE under Section 504. Following OCR's intervention, the district agreed to conduct an IEP meeting to discuss the parents' concerns regarding the implementation of the IEP and to provide specific notice to the student's teachers of the obligation to implement it. The district also agreed to convene a meeting between the parents and the student's teachers in the new school year to ensure the terms of the IEP were being appropriately implemented.

Transportation Services

- **OCR initiated a** proactive investigation to determine whether a large school district failed to provide students with disabilities with transportation to and from the locations where they were receiving educational services. In its resolution with OCR, the district agreed to ensure that students with disabilities received the needed transportation services by taking the following steps: publicizing and operating a phone system to promptly trouble-shoot transportation issues; maintaining a system for reporting monthly on transportation problems and their resolution; notifying parents of their right to reimbursement for the costs of getting their children to school; determining if students who miss school time due to transportation failures are entitled to compensatory education; and providing relevant training for school principals.

• **OCR initiated a** statewide investigation of whether children who rode buses specifically for students with disabilities were inappropriately receiving a shorter school day and less instructional time compared to students without disabilities who did not ride special transport. To settle this case with OCR, the state agreed to implement new, statewide standards for ensuring that students with disabilities on these bus routes were not receiving a shortened school day because of a district's transportation schedule; conduct audits of school districts' transportation schedules and appoint a coordinator responsible for ensuring that districts take corrective steps; require districts to create tracking systems for buses; and monitor districts' implementation of the tracking systems.

Discipline

Students with disabilities are disproportionately disciplined in comparison to their peers without disabilities. For example, OCR's Civil Rights Data Collection shows that students served by IDEA are twice as likely to be suspended out

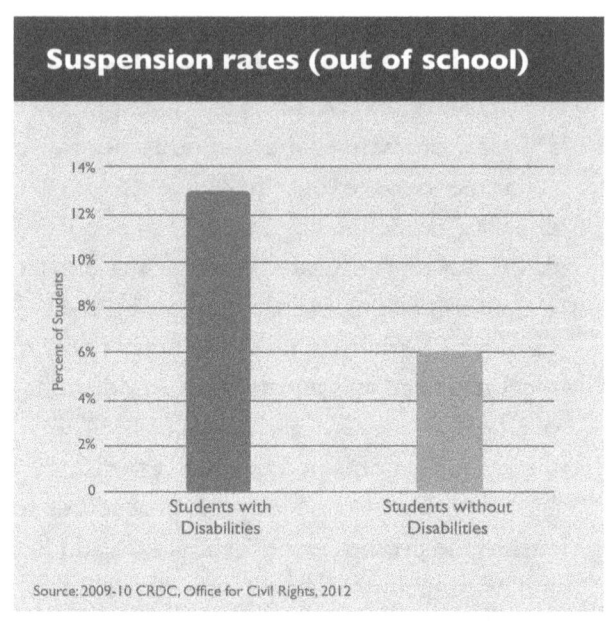

Suspension rates (out of school)

Source: 2009-10 CRDC, Office for Civil Rights, 2012

of school as their peers without disabilities. In Fiscal Years 2009–11, OCR received over 750 complaints alleging disability discrimination concerning discipline.

OCR works to protect students with disabilities from violation of their rights in the discipline process. Under Section 504 and Title II, students with disabilities may not be punished or disciplined for behavior that is caused by or is a manifestation of their disabilities. To protect against this, schools must hold a hearing before suspending a student with a disability for more than 10 cumulative days during a school year.

Additionally, students with disabilities must not be subjected to discriminatorily different treatment in discipline, and must not be disciplined more harshly or frequently than similarly situated students without disabilities for the same infractions.

One example of OCR's work in disability

discipline issues involved a parent who alleged that a school district had indefinitely suspended her son with Asperger's Syndrome without a hearing. The child had brought a container of harmless materials to school that the school mistakenly perceived as a safety risk. The parent further alleged that the school had neither promptly evaluated and placed her son nor provided him special education or related services in this matter. OCR facilitated an agreement between the parent and the school district in which the district agreed to expedite the FAPE and discipline hearing processes; allow the student to return to a different high school in the district, with transportation, and retake some courses; provide information to the district attorney to assist in dropping criminal charges; and conduct an internal review of how it was handling this type of situation.

Academic Adjustments for Postsecondary Students

Postsecondary institutions also have critical obligations to students with disabilities. Students with disabilities who meet the academic and technical standards for admission to, or participation in, the program are entitled to academic modifications (such as course substitutions or additional time for completing degree requirements) and auxiliary aids and services (such as screen readers or sign language interpreters) to ensure their equal opportunity to participate in the program. A postsecondary student with a disability who wishes to receive academic modifications or auxiliary aids and services (sometimes referred to collectively as "accommodations") must inform the college of the disability and need for accommodation.

Colleges do not have to make changes to academic requirements that they can demonstrate are essential to the instruction being pursued, nor do they have to provide academic adjustments that they can demonstrate would fundamentally alter the institution's program or would result in undue financial or administrative burdens. Short of meeting this high bar, however, the costs of providing auxiliary aids and services are not valid reasons for failing to provide the aids or services.

Enforcement: Academic Adjustments

In Fiscal Years 2009–11, OCR received over 1,500 complaints alleging violations concerning academic adjustments for students with disabilities. These complaints frequently involved disputes over what types of academic adjustments the postsecondary institution would provide the student and whether the adjustments were being adequately provided. Following are some of the issues OCR has addressed regarding such adjustments:

• **A college failed** to provide sign language interpreters to students with hearing impairments. Because of a shortage of interpreters, the college videotaped some classes and had students with hearing impairments make appointments with interpreters to review the videos, while still requiring the students to attend classes even though there was no interpreter. Some students with hearing impairments found the videos to be ineffective: scheduling a separate appointment with the interpreter took too much time; the video was going too fast for the student to ask the interpreter questions; and students could not ask the teacher questions while watching the videotape because the teacher was not present. In its resolution with OCR, the college agreed to hire one new part-time interpreter; review its entire interpreting system to determine how to meet its current needs; and offer affected students the options of retroactively dropping classes, obtaining refunds and repeating courses.

• **A student alleged** that his college discriminated against him by dismissing him from its medical office technology program based on his HIV-positive status. One course required students to draw blood from each other, and the college had expressed safety concerns. To resolve the complaint, the college agreed to offer re-enrollment to the student, consider his request for the academic adjustment of not having other students draw his blood, and develop and provide training on procedures to address academic adjustment requests.

• **A deaf student** in a college's teacher education program needed a sign language interpreter for student teaching. College officials told her that if she used an interpreter she might not meet state technical standards for teaching and might not pass her student teaching requirement. The college provided inconsistent interpreter services and did not make improvements after the student complained. After the state department of education clarified that there was no state position on whether the use of interpreters during student teaching affected a student's eligibility for teacher certification, the college agreed with OCR to consistently provide the student with qualified interpreters, to not consider her use of an interpreter in evaluating her student teaching, and to generally provide students with appropriate accommodations.

Accessibility of Technology

Technology plays an increasingly important role in education at all levels. For example, schools and colleges commonly use computers in traditional classrooms; electronic book readers that supplement or replace paper textbooks; online classes; and online registration and class scheduling. Section 504 and Title II require schools and colleges to ensure that the technology they use is fully accessible to individuals with disabilities or to otherwise provide equal access to the educational benefits and opportunities afforded by the technology.

Policy: Accessibility of Technology

In 2010, the Department issued groundbreaking policy guidance with the Department of Justice on how Section 504 and the ADA apply to emerging technologies, especially electronic book readers, in education. The guidance, set forth in a letter addressed to college and university presidents, makes clear that if an emerging technology is inaccessible to students who are blind, then requiring the use of that technology in a classroom is prohibited by Section 504 and the ADA. This prohibition is lifted when schools and colleges provide blind students with accommodations or modifications that permit them to receive all the educational benefits of the program in an equally effective and equally integrated manner. Such accommodations allow blind students to acquire the same information, engage in the same interactions and enjoy the same services as sighted students. In 2011, the Department issued a follow-up document explaining that the principles underlying the 2010 guidance also apply to elementary and secondary schools; to students with other disabilities, such as learning disabilities, that affect the ability to access printed materials; and to other forms of online or emerging technology beyond electronic book readers.

Additionally, OCR's assistant secretary furthered the goal of accessible technology serving as a commissioner on the Advisory Commission on Accessible Instructional Materials in Postsecondary Education for Students with Disabilities (AIM Commission), created by Congress to study and make recommendations to improve the ability of postsecondary students with disabilities to obtain accessible instructional materials in a timely and cost-effective manner. The AIM Commission issued its report in December 2011, urging Congress to, among other things, authorize the United States Access Board to set guidelines for accessible instructional materials and offer incentives for innovation in the development of such materials.[5]

Enforcement: Accessibility of Technology

As the use of technology in education increases, OCR's enforcement efforts are ensuring that students with disabilities have the same opportunities as students without disabilities in this fast-changing area. OCR has initiated two proactive reviews to ensure that schools, colleges and universities are not using technology in a way that discriminates against students with disabilities. OCR has also addressed complaints in this area, such as the following:

- **Working with a** private company, a university established a pilot program to provide students with electronic book readers with Web browsers as a source of class-related, text-based information. Advocacy organizations alleged that the electronic book reader was not accessible to blind and visually impaired students, and that alternate formats did not provide these students with equal access. After OCR and the Department of Justice began investigating, the university agreed to require, purchase or incorporate electronic book readers into its programs only if the readers were fully accessible to students with visual impairments. Alternatively, the university also agreed to provide a reasonable modification or accommodation that would allow students with visual impairments to access and acquire the same information, engage in the same interactions and enjoy the same services as sighted students in their classes.

- **Online colleges,** like their brick-and-mortar counterparts, must not discriminate against students with disabilities. OCR has seen an increase in complaints filed against online colleges in recent years. In one case, for example, a student alleged that an online college did not properly accommodate her disabilities

(including bipolar disorder and chronic pain syndrome) to allow her to access its paralegal training program. In particular, the student wanted extra time to complete assignments and tests. OCR found that the college did not have an adequate process for students with disabilities to request academic adjustments or accommodations. The college agreed to fully refund the student's tuition; develop a new policy on academic adjustments and auxiliary aids and services, as well as a revised grievance procedure to provide for the prompt and equitable resolution of Section 504 issues; and publicize the new policies and procedures and train all staff on them.

- **A college student** with a disability withdrew from an online math class because he could not use his testing accommodation, extra time, for the online tests. The software did not allow for untimed testing, and the professor would have had to spend about 50 minutes converting each test into a format that would work for untimed situations. The college required the student with a disability to come in to the testing center during specified hours and take a test on paper, while the other students in the class could take the test online, from anywhere, at any time during a 48-hour window. OCR found that the online program did not provide equal access given that the student with a disability did not have the same ease of use and ready access to the test as other students. The additional work it would have taken to prepare an untimed online version of each test was not an undue burden. Following OCR's intervention, the college reimbursed the student for the cost of the course, cancelled its collection action for unpaid tuition, notified credit agencies and trained its staff on accommodations.

Physical Accessibility of Programs, Services and Facilities

OCR is committed to ensuring that persons with disabilities have physical access to the programs, services and facilities of schools and colleges. Parts of old buildings may need to be renovated, and new buildings need to be properly constructed so that individuals with disabilities, including those who use wheelchairs, can, among other things, enter and navigate, use bathrooms, and park near the buildings.

Enforcement: Accessibility of Programs, Services and Facilities

In Fiscal Years 2009–11, OCR received over 500 complaints alleging violations in the accessibility of programs, services and facilities, and initiated three proactive reviews on this topic. Following are some of the issues OCR has addressed in this area:

- **OCR conducted a** proactive review of accessibility at a university campus and found compliance problems with, among other things, the slope and size of parking spaces; the doors and shelves in bathrooms; the slope of a ramp in a building; the pressure required to open some classroom doors; and routes blocked by obstacles such as trash cans and picnic tables. The college agreed to correct these problems.

- **In another proactive** accessibility review of a college, OCR found several concerns. The university agreed to remedy these concerns with the following measures: (1) providing accessible restrooms in identified buildings and facilities; (2) providing accessible seating in the campus basketball facility and football coliseum; (3) installing audible alarms in the campus auditorium building; (4) providing accessible parking on campus; (5) identifying an accessible pedestrian route on campus and providing notice of the route to the public; and (6) installing appropriate accessibility signage on all building and facility entrances.

- **A complaint alleged** that elementary school playgrounds within a school district were not accessible for individuals with mobility disabilities. OCR negotiated an agreement in which the district committed to spending $2.2 million over eight years to make all the elementary school playgrounds accessible for individuals with mobility disabilities.

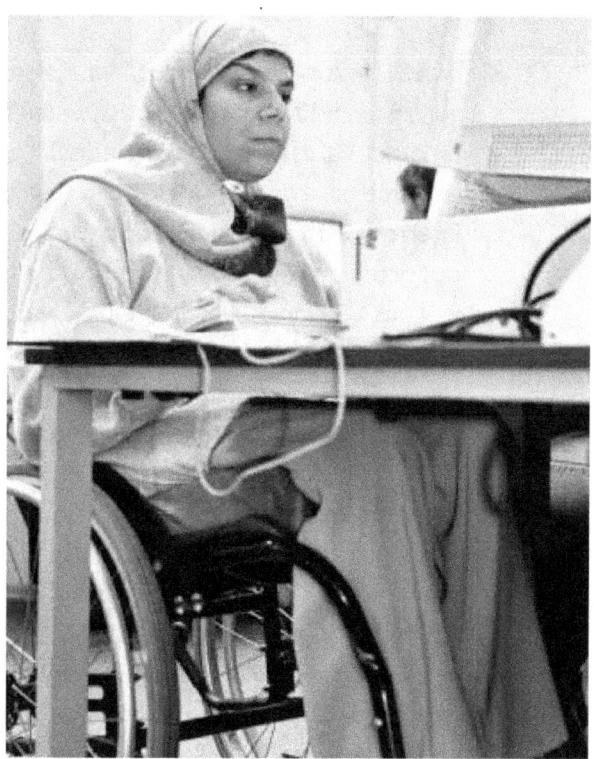

Preventing and Addressing Harassment, Including Bullying That Rises to the Level of Harassment

Students with disabilities have the right to be educated free from harassment and bullying based on their disability. Harassment can have severe educational, emotional and physical effects on the harassed students and their peers, whether at the K–12 or postsecondary level. Harassing conduct may take many forms, including bullying and name-calling, graphic and written statements, or other kinds of physical or verbal conduct that may be threatening, harmful or humiliating. OCR seeks to eradicate discriminatory harassment and create environments in which all students, including students with disabilities, are safe to learn.

Policy Guidance: Harassment

The Department issued groundbreaking policy guidance in 2010 explaining that when bullying or other harassment based on disability creates a hostile environment serious enough to limit or interfere with a student's ability to benefit from opportunities offered by a school, the harassment violates Section 504 and Title II. If an institution knows, or has reason to know, about student-on-student harassment, Section 504 and Title II require that schools take immediate and effective action to eliminate the harassment, prevent its recurrence, and, where appropriate, address its effects on the harassed student and the school community. OCR's policy guidance provides examples of harassment and how a school should respond. The policy guidance also addresses harassment based on race, color, national origin

and sex, which are covered by other laws OCR enforces. For more information about this area of our work, please refer to Title VI Enforcement Highlights and Title IX Enforcement Highlights. Both documents can be found at: http://www2.ed.gov/about/offices/list/ocr/publications.html.

Enforcement: Harassment

In Fiscal Years 2009–11, OCR received over 1,000 complaints of disability harassment. Following are some of the issues raised and resolutions achieved:

- **A complainant alleged** that a high school student with Fragile X Syndrome, Asperger's Syndrome, Tourette's Syndrome and ADHD was verbally ridiculed by her fellow students about her disability-related body odor, sprayed with an air freshener by staff in front of her classmates, detained by staff in school who made her take showers before allowing her to attend classes, and pulled out of class to be sent home before the end of the school day because of her body odor. She wanted to drop out because of the harassment. OCR facilitated an Early Complaint Resolution agreement in which the school district agreed to provide training to staff about the student's disabilities and Section 504 and Title II; enroll the student in its "Senior Life Skills" course; provide the student with weekly social work services; and assist the student in obtaining a community job.

- **Parents alleged that** their child with cerebral palsy, scoliosis and ADD, who weighed only 65 pounds, was bullied and harassed by classmates at middle school and on the school bus. They said he was kicked in the legs in the cafeteria, intentionally hit in the head while playing dodgeball, and hit with bottles at a pep rally. As a result, the parents removed the child from school to home-school him. OCR facilitated an Early Complaint Resolution in which the school agreed to set up a hotline for the complainant to use to report future concerns; train staff; fully implement policies and procedures on bullying and harassment; discipline students who engaged in bullying and harassing; and report incidents to parents in a timely manner.

• **A parent complained** that a student with a severe nut allergy was the subject of a protest instigated by district employees because of aids and services provided to the student to address her food allergy. The complainant alleged that several teachers, including a teacher who had been reprimanded for failing to implement the aids and services, leaked confidential information about the student's medical condition and spread misinformation about the accommodations to other parents, and that an online response to a news story concerning the protest included a suggestion that parents send their children to school with backpacks smeared in peanut oil, which could have proved fatal for her child. OCR obtained a resolution in which the district agreed, among other things, to revise its anti-harassment policy and grievance procedures; educate students, faculty, staff and the community about the severity of nut allergies and the need for appropriate aids and services in schools; provide compensatory education or other services to the student who was harassed; and give the student the choice of transferring schools.

Right to Equal Treatment

Under Section 504 and Title II, OCR works to ensure equal treatment for students with disabilities. Section 504 and Title II prohibit treating students with disabilities differently on the basis of disability unless doing so is necessary to provide those students with an equal opportunity to participate in, and receive the benefits of, an institution's programs. This applies to such areas as admissions and recruitment; college and university housing; access to college and career-ready courses; access to nonacademic and extracurricular activities, including extracurricular athletics; retaliation against those who report Section 504 and Title II violations; and employment.

Enforcement: Equal Treatment

OCR investigates allegations of different treatment of students with disabilities and addresses allegations of the denial of access to academic programs and extracurricular activities. Following are examples of such allegations:

• **When the parents** of a student with autism wished to enroll him in his elementary school's after-school child-care program, the school required the parents to pay for a one-to-one aide and a behaviorist for the student, even though the school determined that the student needed these services to receive FAPE during the school day. Following OCR's investigation, the school district agreed to reimburse parents and guardians who paid for the provision of aids or services to enable children with disabilities to participate in the after-school child care program. It also agreed to revise its policies and practices so that students with disabilities who need aids or services to participate in the program are not denied admission on that basis and are not charged for these aids or services.

- **A school failed** to provide adequate notice of extracurricular activities to students with disabilities in a self-contained high school class. Also, those students were regularly unable to participate in pep rallies because of their busing arrangements. OCR obtained an agreement in which the school district will provide students with disabilities equal access to information about all extracurricular activities and will ensure that students with disabilities are not excluded from pep rallies.

- **A university required** a student with reflex sympathetic dystrophy to pay a surcharge for the double dormitory room without a roommate that she received as an accommodation for her disability. OCR obtained a resolution in which the university agreed to reimburse the student for the surcharge and to revise its room rate policy so that students with disabilities are not required to pay surcharges for dormitory rooms received as accommodations.

The Transformed Civil Rights Data Collection: New Information to Improve Compliance With Section 504 and Title II

Information and transparency about disparities in educational opportunities and resources are powerful tools to aid in the effort to improve schools. The most recent Civil Rights Data Collection (CRDC), released in March 2012 with data from the 2009–10 school year, includes many new indicators on the educational experiences of students with disabilities. The data cover topics such as high school course offerings, course-taking, restraint and seclusion, bullying and harassment, and discipline at the school and district levels.

While the 2009–10 CRDC data cover about 85 percent of the nation's public school students, the CRDC for 2011–12 school year, which will be released in 2013, will include every public school in the nation.

Following are some of the key findings for students with disabilities from the current CRDC:

Demographics

- **One out of** eight students in the CRDC sample (12 percent) has a disability: 4.7 million are served under IDEA and 400,000 are covered by Section 504 only.
- **While about half** of the students without disabilities are male, 67 percent of students served under IDEA, and 63 percent of students covered by Section 504 only, were male.
- **Eighteen percent of** students not covered by IDEA are African-American, while 21 percent of students served under IDEA are African-American.

Bullying and Harassment

- **Out of the** 6,835 districts in the sample, nearly a third (30 percent of districts or 2,048 total districts) reported at least one incident of bullying or harassment on the basis of disability.
- **10,396 students** were reported to have been bullied or harassed on the basis of disability.

Discipline

- **Although only 11 percent** of students overall were served by IDEA, 16 percent of all the students who were expelled in 2009-2010 were served by IDEA.
- **While 21 percent** of students served by IDEA were African-American, 40 percent of those IDEA students who were expelled were African-American.

Restraint and Seclusion

- **Students with disabilities** (those served under IDEA and under Section 504 only) represent 12 percent of students in the sample, but nearly 70 percent of the students who were physically restrained by adults in their schools.
- **African-American students** represent 21 percent of students with disabilities under the IDEA but 44 percent of such students who were subjected to mechanical restraint.

Access to College- and Career-Preparatory Classes

- **Taking Algebra:** Of the IDEA students taking Algebra I in 2009–10, 13 percent took the course in 11th or 12th grade, although it is preferable to take the course earlier to allow students to move to more advanced subjects during later years in high school. Of the non-IDEA students taking Algebra I in 2009–10, only 6 percent did so in these last years of their high school careers.
- **Passing Algebra:** While 79 percent of students without disabilities passed Algebra I in 2009–10, only 68 percent of students served under IDEA successfully passed the course.
- **Retained** (or "held back") one year: Students covered by IDEA represent 11 percent of high school enrollment but 19 percent of students retained in high school (grades 9–12).
- **Taking Physics:** Students served under IDEA make up 11 percent of the high school population but only 4 percent of the students enrolled in physics in 2009–10.

While data alone cannot be a substitute for the thorough investigation necessary to establish violations of civil rights laws, this wealth of new data can help schools, districts and communities deepen their self-analysis and understanding of where change is needed.

Endnotes

1 Section 504 also prohibits disability discrimination in programs and activities conducted by the federal government. OCR does not have authority to enforce this aspect of Section 504. The Department's Office of Management has this authority.

2 Title III of the ADA prohibits disability discrimination by private entities, including private schools, colleges and universities. The Department of Justice enforces Title III. Information about Title III can be found on the Department of Justice website at www.ada.gov.

3 Each federal fiscal year runs from October of one calendar year through September of the next. For example, "fiscal year 2011" or "FY 2011" began Oct. 1, 2010, and ended Sept. 30, 2011.

4 *Helping the Student with Diabetes Succeed: A Guide for School Personnel* (September 2010), available on the National Diabetes Education Program's website at http://ndep.nih.gov/publications/PublicationDetail.aspx?PubId=97&redirect=true#main.

5 *Report of the Advisory Commission on Accessible Instructional Materials in Postsecondary Education for Students with Disabilities* (Dec. 6, 2011), available on the Department's website at http://www2.ed.gov/about/bdscomm/list/aim/publications.html.

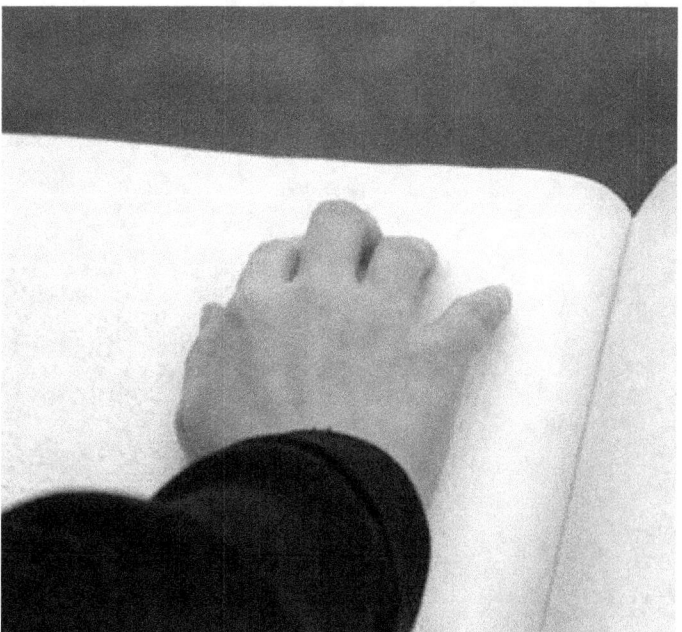

www.ingramcontent.com/pod-product-compliance
Lightning Source LLC
Chambersburg PA
CBHW052029280526
45793CB00005B/1178